KINGDONOMICS
FROM LIVING IN THE HOOD TO EATING THE GOOD

Rondy Long Jr

*All scriptures are from the **King James Version** of the Bible unless otherwise noted.*

First published by Last Generation Publishing 2025

Copyright © 2025 by Rondy Long

All rights reserved. No part of this publication may be reproduced, stored or transmitted in any form or by any means, electronic, mechanical, photocopying, recording, scanning, or otherwise without written permission from the publisher. It is illegal to copy this book, post it to a website, or distribute it by any other means without permission.

First edition
ISBN: 979-8-9869734-7-0

This book was professionally typeset on Last Generation Publishing.

Find out more at lastgenerationpublishing.com

LastGenerationPublishing.com

Table of Contents

Chapter 1: Craving Polo Prosperity 3

Chapter 2: Living in the Hood 9

Chapter 3: Nothing Happens Financially Good in the Hood 15

Chapter 4: Willing & Obedient 33

Chapter 5: Willing and Obedient = WO? 41

Chapter 6: What is Kingdomnomics? 55

Chapter 7: Faith or Foolishness? 71

Prosperity Scripture Confessions 79

Appendix

Why We Believe in Prosperity 87

What I'm Believing For 101

What I Owe 105

Kingdonomics Chart 121

Salvation 123

Last Generation Publishing 125

Author 127

Chapter 1 | Kingdonomics

Craving Polo Prosperity

It was Tuesday, August 21, the first day of school for my 8th grade year. I hopped on that white Metro Bus with red and blue stripes, ready to embark on a new adventure. The ride was always a bit bumpy rolling down Belfort or MLK Drive in the hood since the city officials, who were black folks, were always elected but never fixed our streets. But that didn't faze me. I was filled with a thrilling sense of anticipation for the year ahead.

Let me introduce myself. My name is Rondy Long. The year was 1984 and I was just an unknown Black boy growing up in South Park, Houston.

The world around me pulsed with energy and possibility. Everywhere I turned, there were reminders of the cultural zeitgeist. Kevin Bacon's rebellious dance moves in *Footloose*, Prince's funk-infused *Purple Rain*, the Cosby Show's portrayal of a successful Black family, and Michael Jackson's *Thriller* album had the nation mesmerized. Yet beneath those exciting distractions, a deeper calling was beginning to stir within me, a path that would eventually lead me to the pulpit as a teenage preacher. But for now, I was still captivated by the creativity and bold energy of the 80s.

My social status back then was what you might call in-between. I wasn't very popular, but I was known by all the cool kids. Not the most talented, but I ended up winning the talent show that year. Not super good-looking, but some girls called me cute. I guess I had a certain "je ne sais quoi" because I always had my crew of friends.

Being an in-between kid meant I didn't have the trendiest clothes. No Sony Walkman, just a trusty Sanyo cassette player. No flashy K-Swiss or Fila sneakers, but I was perfectly content in my own style. There was one brand I did crave though—Polo by Ralph Lauren. In the 80s, the preppy look was all the rage and Polo represented elegance and status. As Ralph Lauren said, "I don't design clothes. I design dreams."

Ah, those carefree, halcyon days of the 1980s. Let me tell you, anyone worth their salt knew that donning a Ralph Lauren Polo shirt was the surest sign of prosperity. Heck, some shirts even had just the iconic RL initials—the same as mine, would you believe it? But alas, my dear mother could never afford the genuine article. Instead, she would scour the markets for USPA or Knights of the Round Table knock-offs, the ones with the man on the horse waving the flag.

Now, in my neck of the woods, the cool kids had a game called "ranking." My mom's generation knew it as "playing the dozens," and while the youngsters these days call it "roasting." The unwritten rule was simple. Show up in a fake Polo and you were fair game to be roasted until kingdom come.

But that particular first day of school, I was ready to take the world by storm. I had a genuine pink Ralph Lauren Polo with the famous green emblem. I'll never forget the moment I pulled it from the bag. It smelled like money. It smelled cool. It smelled like a girl magnet. Yes sir, Ralph Lauren wasn't just selling clothes, he was selling a lifestyle, and I was about to live it large! That shirt sparked my first desire for a better life. The abundant life. The prosperous life.

As the bus rolled on, jostling me in my seat, I felt a sense of nervous excitement. This would be a year of adventure and discovering my own unique path. Who knew what exciting opportunities lay ahead? I gripped the edge of my seat, ready to take on the world.

I remember that day vividly, as if it were yesterday. Stepping off the bus, full of excitement and anticipation, clutching my new backpack, ready to show off my fresh new look. I had picked out that pink Polo shirt with such care, convinced it would earn me instant cool points from my peers.

But instead of the back-slapping and "attaboys" I had imagined, I was met with laughter and relentless teasing. The source of their amusement? The matching pink polyester pants my mom had bought to go with the Polo. Oh, the horror! Pink polyester pants from Montgomery Ward... a JCPenney knock-off. The pants had to be hemmed. They were stiff, ill-fitting, and church-slacks-gone-wrong. A far cry from the revered Levi's 501s that ruled the fashion scene.

I felt embarrassed and let down. I had tried my best to fit in, to be one of the cool kids, only to be cruelly singled out for my sartorial misstep. As an in-betweener, I was always walking a fine line, desperate to earn that elusive stamp of approval, but always falling just short due to some nagging imperfection.

I can still remember the sting of my friends' taunts, how they ruthlessly "tore me up" over those pants. It took months before I could wear that Polo again. And those pants? Well, they were swiftly banished to the back of my closet, never to see the light of day.

Looking back, I can laugh about it now. But in that moment, it felt like the end of the world. The harsh reality of trying to navigate the treacherous waters of adolescent social dynamics. A rite of passage, in its own way, that we all endure. And though the scars may fade, the memory of that day will always be etched in my mind.

Chapter 2 | Kingdonomics
Living in the Hood

Whoa, have I ever lived in the hood? You bet I have! Growing up, I spent a good chunk of my life in some pretty rough neighborhoods. But you know what? There's so much more to the hood than what you see in movies or hear in hip-hop songs.

The hood can be a tough environment, you know? There are lots of challenges and lots of distractions. If you've ever watched the movie, *Boyz n the Hood*, you saw what my neighborhood looked like, sounded like, and felt like. It was all houses, some definitely funded by government housing. I'm sure it wasn't as bad as hood apartment living, but it was bad. And yet, it was also good.

You had very few husbands and wives. Some grandparents were raising kids. A lot of single moms, and even closeted gay couples, called the hood home. There were drugs and some gang activity, definitely not to the extent of Los Angeles, but still plenty of challenges: poverty, crime, lack of opportunity. There were booming car systems, pretty girls, and muscle-bound Black boys. Lots of potentially pro athletes, most of whom would be killed, imprisoned, or drop out of high school before they could be discovered.

I remember vividly the sounds of the hood: trains rumbling down the tracks, police sirens speeding to the scene of a crime, hip-hop thumping from someone's 1977 Cutlass—Run DMC's "Sucker MCs" or a Darryl Scott mixtape. Kids playing hot ball in the streets or neighborhood kickball. Dutiful neighbors mowing lawns or washing cars. And that low hum of industrial factories or nearby construction crews.

But not just the sounds—what about the smells? Bacon or sausage wafting from most houses in the morning. And on celebration days in Houston, Texas, you could smell barbecue. The wood-smoked brisket, ribs, and sausage drifting for miles on days like July 4th, Easter, high school graduations, even Christmas. Houston had a lot of migrants from Louisiana, so every winter you'd catch the aroma of Creole gumbo.

Walking down neighborhood streets, there were other familiar smells: Clorox and Ajax on Saturday mornings as Black mommas made everyone get up and clean. Soap from freshly hung clothes on backyard clotheslines. Fresh-cut grass from Mr. Wilson, who trimmed his yard like clockwork every Saturday morning in spring and summer. And more nefarious scents too—someone smoking weed, discarded alcohol, and the faint smell of urine that lingered near some homes.

Oddly, I also remember the smell of what I'd later learn were chemtrails. Maybe it was mosquito repellent. Maybe it was something those planes were releasing when they flew overhead. But it definitely wasn't natural.

My memories of the hood are a mixed bag. There were good ones and bad ones. It's where I learned to fix my bike and pop wheelies. It's also where I experienced physical and sexual abuse by my caregiver. It's where I learned how to get in a three-point stance for football, and where an older boy once tried to rape me on the way to church, and I barely escaped. It's where I learned to fight, but also where I got jumped and beat up more than a few times.

Sure, there were challenges. But there was also resilience, a sense of community, and a whole lot of heart. There are people in the hood who need Jesus, and people who already have Him on their side. I've met some of the most amazing, faithful people who call the hood home. They were fighting to make their communities better one day at a time.

And here's the thing. You can graduate from the hood.

I know hip-hop often preaches about keeping it real and staying in the neighborhood, but I have my own views. I believe that sometimes you need to move on to pursue new opportunities and grow. Staying in the hood forever isn't always the best choice for everyone. In my experience, when you begin to advance and make progress, you might need to consider leaving. It's not about abandoning your roots or turning your back. It's about expanding your horizons and opening up new doors for yourself and your family.

I remember when I finally made the decision to leave. It was scary, but exhilarating. I broke the cycle. Got an education. Built a better life for myself, my wife, and my children.

The one thing everyone had in common in the hood? No one ever had enough money. Not one person. Money was always the main focus—how to get it, keep it, use it, flaunt it. This hunger for financial freedom is what fuels excellence in Black athletics and entertainment. All those stories—they're all rags to riches.

Pick any famous Black Mike: Mike Tyson, Mike Jordan, Mike Jackson, Mike Vick—they all came from poverty. That hunger drove their greatness. Fred Hammond, the Winans, the Wayans, Venus and Serena Williams, the Clark Sisters. We may not fully endorse every person, sacred or secular, but the truth remains. Growing up in the hood without enough money created the drive to be great. To do something. To reach for abundance and prosperity.

Because for some people, the hood and its poverty create the greatest desire and the fiercest opportunity to rise.

Chapter 3 | Kingdonomics
Nothing Happens Financially Good In the Hood

Have you ever watched an episode of *Good Times*? JJ, James, Florida, Thelma, and Michael…"Good Times…keeping your head above water, making a way when you can…" Nothing was truly good about *Good Times*. They always "almost" got out of the hood—but they never did. It was as if a spirit kept holding them back. That's exactly what it's like in the hood. Like the show, it was often their own decisions that kept them stuck. But it also felt like something deeper, like a spirit nudging them toward poor choices.

Like the guy who was ready to go to a D-1 college on a full-ride football scholarship to play football and then likely head out for the pros. But the summer he was supposed to leave for college, he commits a robbery and goes to jail, or goes to the wrong party and gets killed in random drive by, or gets in a drunk driving accident and is permanently disabled.

The hood is full of stories like these—of people replete with opportunity, who almost certainly should have made it out, but never did.

And then there are the ones who *did* get out but never got the hood *out* of them. Think of Michael Vick—the football player who "kept it real" by surrounding himself with childhood friends, continuing hood activities until he landed in jail for illegal dogfighting.

It makes you want to say, like the theme song of *The Beverly Hillbillies*, "C'mon Jed, move away from there." There's a strong spirit that governs the hood, like the song *Hotel California*: "You can check out any time you like, but you can never leave."

Here are some of the top things I believe the poverty spirit uses to keep people poor in the hood:

- Dependence on government social programming
- Sexual immorality
- Social justice efforts that normalize or decriminalize crime (drug dealing, theft, drug use)
- Financial predators who had access to "easy money" rip off
- Poverty theology

I never knew a time when I wasn't indoctrinated by my mom's views that Republicans were white prejudiced bigots who hated Black people and didn't want to help our community. Democrats, I was told, loved Black people and always supported programs that helped us.

Growing up, I trusted what my mom told me about politics. I believed Democrats were the ones who truly cared and wanted to uplift our communities. It seemed like they fought for us and offered real assistance. I must admit—some liberal Democrat policies did help people in the hood, including me.

But as I gained more life experience and began thinking critically, I realized that much of the "help" being offered was not as beneficial as I had been led to believe. In many cases, those policies were causing more harm than good.

Coming to this realization was hard. It went against everything I had been taught. I had to re-examine my beliefs and challenge the narrative I'd grown up with.

As someone who grew up in ghetto neighborhoods, I can say that government programs like food stamps, Section 8, welfare, and Medicaid were a real help to me and many others. I'm not sure whether we truly needed them to survive, or if we simply used them because they were readily available and culturally normalized. Either way, I know there was a time when my wife and I benefited from some of those programs.

Food stamps helped us for about six months while I was in between jobs and didn't earn enough to support my family. Medicaid was a lifesaver when our children were born and for their pediatric care over the years. So, when I critique these programs as mechanisms of poverty, I speak from personal experience.

I'm not saying all of these programs need to be gutted. But I do believe they should be transitional in nature. Families who remain on assistance for decades—or across generations—should be transitioned into job training and career placement programs.

I've consistently noticed that in neighborhoods with high levels of government assistance like Section 8 and food stamps, there's often elevated drug and criminal activity. When there's no incentive to work because housing and food are provided, it breeds idle time—which can easily lead to drug use, dealing, and even sexual abuse of children.

I know these programs can be a lifeline, but I believe they must be structured to encourage self-sufficiency and break cycles of poverty—rather than perpetuate them. It's complex. But it's personal.

As I walk through the neighborhood, I can't help but notice the grown men riding bicycles up and down the streets. These are men who should be out working and providing for themselves or their households, but instead they seem to be living off the system.

I can't help but wonder, how are they able to maintain this lifestyle without holding down a steady job? The sad reality is that they are likely living off the income of a woman, who is probably working multiple jobs and relying on government assistance like Section 8 housing, food stamps, Medicaid, and welfare to make ends meet.

These men are unofficial residents, crashing with their girlfriends, mothers, grandmothers, or other family members and friends. Many of them have criminal records, have just been released from incarceration, or can't keep a job because of drug addiction.

It's a heartbreaking cycle of poverty, crime, and government dependency. The drugs, crime, and even sexual assault that plague these neighborhoods are in a sense government-funded, as the system fails to provide the support and resources these communities desperately need. Or in another sense the system helps "too much", and our young men who are potential heads of families (fathers and husbands) experience arrested development.

Sexual Immorality

Most people don't attach poverty and sexual immorality. But they are very closely related. Many black women of the 60's and 70's chose to marry Uncle Sam rather than a husband. Why? Because the government incentivized black women fornicating with men, having babies out of wedlock, to ensure government welfare funding.

I'm going to provide some historical context regarding President Lyndon B. Johnson's policies in the late 1960s. Johnson implemented several social programs, including AFDC, welfare, food stamps, and housing assistance. These initiatives were intended to garner support among African American and minority voters, as he believed they would secure Democratic votes for decades.

He said in a statement that if he created these social programs, "we will have N----rs (black people) voting for democrats for the next 50 years!"

However, the impact of these programs has been significant. Critics argue that they unintentionally discouraged traditional family structures. For instance, the design of these benefits created incentives for single motherhood, as financial assistance was often contingent on the absence of a male partner in the household.

At the time Johnson initiated these policies, approximately 35% of African American women were single. Today, nearly 70% of African American women are single, and a substantial number of children are being raised in single-parent households. This shift raises important questions about the long-term effects of these social programs on family dynamics and community structures.

So now, the more sexual immorality our young women in the hood participate in and get pregnant without a husband or man in the house, the more government resources they could get. Even in the late 1960s, social programming required that the man be removed from the house. If you watch the 1970's movie, Claudine, featuring James Earl Jones, you will find what I'm saying is true. Most people don't connect the dots between poverty and sexual sins. But a single mom makes $20,000 to $40,000 less than her female peer without children and $50,000 to $100,000 less than her married peer with combined income accompanying a husband. She makes less money, has more expenses, and is almost always forced to use government assistance which dis-incentivizes her getting married, making more money, or upward mobility. If she begins to make too much money, Uncle Sam will cut her off. So, she's just stuck until she turns her back on her current husband, "Uncle Sam," and embraces morality i.e. marriage. Her children are also stuck in a cycle of poverty because they are living in drug/crime-ridden neighborhoods, with negative influences, under-emphasized educational environment, combined with academically failing schools. Her daughters will almost always repeat history as far as teen pregnancy, and her sons will probably repeat the pattern of their fathers with multiple children by multiple women. With no male guidance in the home, many of the boys will end up dead or imprisoned. If a young man or woman living in the hood can avoid children out of wedlock, they will definitely increase their chances of prosperity and abundance.

Even Barack Obama declared the truth about how fornication and single parent moms affected the economics of the hood. Listen to what Barack Obama said.:

"You and I know how true this is in the African-American community. We know that more than half of all black children live in single-parent households, a number that has doubled – doubled – since we were children. We know the statistics – that children who grow up without a father are five times more likely to live in poverty and commit crime; nine times more likely to drop out of schools and twenty times more likely to end up in prison. They are more likely to have behavioral problems, or run away from home, or become teenage parents themselves. And the foundations of our community are weaker because of it."

Social Justice and Decriminalization

This is really a silent killer in the hood. So, liberals like to solve things by not really solving them. Instead of fixing the drug problems, they decided, "just give them clean needles." Instead of lowering crime, like selling and using drugs, they just stop calling it an actual crime, i.e., Let's make using and selling drugs legal. Instead of improving education so that more children can actually pass the S.A.T. and graduate, they lowered the score requirements for minorities and reclassified a "C" grade as a "B" grade, and a "B" grade as an "A+" grade. They just rename the problem, the solution, and that solves it. I've seen this over and over, and it starts in our public schools. The schools need to show a better discipline record in the state. The school is constantly having to arrest and suspend students for fighting. Instead of doing the hard work like teaching conflict resolution and behavior modification, what do the liberals do? They just stop arresting and suspending students for the same type of fighting. Now, it looks like arrest and suspensions for fighting have gone down. Now, they can lie and say fighting has gone down 50% since last year, but this is not true. The school only stopped punishing the fight breakouts and there is now no record of it. So, here is the liberal rhetoric: There are too many young black men in jail. My question is if there are too many young black men committing crimes? Never mind that those same people say things like, "We need to stop the number of black men going to jail!" Liberals always believe the end justifies the means. So, what do we do? Let's decriminalize the crimes they are committing, let's have cashless bail, let's degrade felonies to misdemeanors. Yikes! So, what does this do? Does it lower crime? No! It lowers crime statistics. Now, criminals are more embolden and the hood becomes even more dangerous and deadly. Why? Because criminals become less afraid and deterred by the consequences. Young kids can just walk into Walgreens or CVS, fill their backpack with goods and walk out without consequences if it's under $500. This makes thieves more embolden to rob private citizens.

When the media and Civil Rights leaders make people in the hood perpetual victims, it cements them to be a permanent "underclass." What this signals to the minorities is no matter how hard you try you will never get out. Sounds like Hotel California: "You can check out, but you can never leave." This type of despair and hopelessness is what I grew up hearing and being indoctrinated in. This is why many of my friends went to jail or got killed selling and doing drugs. This is why so many of my young African-American sisters got pregnant. "There is no hope," society says. Then American Hip-Hop came along and sealed the coffin. Hip-hop made thugging, criming, sexing, and drug dealing the Vogue thing to do. This was no longer seen as criminal and negative thing to do, but now these gangster rap dudes, and sex-rap girls became the role models of the hood.

So now, how can lil' Jaquan get a job with tattoos on his face, talking like, looking like, and smelling like a rapper high on weed? He can't. This is what leads to hopelessness. This is where God, the gospel, and Word of Faith came in for me.

The Blame Game

Now, when you live in the "hood," there is a lot of blame to go around for the conditions in the ghetto. This is of 400 years of slavery. "It's the white man oppressing us." People in the hood blame everyone for their conditions: the white man, their traumatic upbringing, their mama, their daddy, lack of opportunity, etc. Rarely do they ever blame their current economic status on themselves. I have told people of every race and color everywhere I go this: *"America is the greatest land for opportunity; If you can't get ahead in America, you can't get ahead anywhere."* People risk their lives to get here, but why? People don't risk their lives to get to China or Russia, why? Because the United States is rich with opportunity. Only in our country could a poor man name Leo who was also discriminated against, put a little piece of cotton on both ends of a little stick, call it a Q-tip, and become a millionaire.

I often tell people in the hood; *it's* time to rise above excuses for poverty and failure. I say all the time that there is no white man, black man, brown man, yellow man, or polka dot man that can stop you when God is with you and you are determined. Let's embrace that truth! After I first got married, I was called to be the Youth Pastor at a predominantly white Presbyterian Church in Carrollton, TX. In a place like North Dallas, in Carrollton, racism thrived, but

I was called there to serve and make a difference. It wasn't always comfortable, but God was with us, and we grew the youth ministry like the church had never seen before!

I thought this was just a fluke, but God did it again. Just ten miles away, I became the youth pastor again at a large church with 3,000 members, and my wife and I were among only two black people there. I encountered racism, but it was just ignorance and not malicious. The pastor, an older man, asked about my heritage, "What tribe are you from in Africa?" He was unaware of the painful history behind such questions. I responded with grace, acknowledging our complex past, I answered, "Because our women were raped and the slaves from different parts of Africa were forced to intermarry, it's hard to know which tribe I'm from."

One crucial lesson I learned is to stop allowing skin color to be an excuse for failure. So often in the "hood"; people show up for job interviews ill-prepared; dressed inappropriately, or get hired and perform subpar, and then cry racism when there are negative outcomes. Most of the time it's not racism at all, it's about attitude and work ethic. If you are willing and obedient, you will reap the rewards!

Blame, blame, blame, it needs to stop. In the '70s, blacks blamed loss of opportunity on lack of education. This was somewhat true. UNICEF had commercials that taught us "a mind is a terrible thing to waste." Today, we celebrate the fact that more Black individuals are graduating than ever before, yet our communities still face hurdles. Remember, education alone isn't the solution; it's about choosing the right path.

You have one incredible life—commit to your journey and make it extraordinary! Our relationship with Christ transcends our racial and cultural heritage or discrimination. Jesus invites us into a kingdom that transcends race and background. He said, "I am the door." To truly step into the fullness of life, we must embrace this invitation.

Let's acknowledge the truth: Jesus wasn't defined by the color of His skin; He was a Middle Eastern man who came to save us all. Regardless of what others might say, His sacrifice for our sins is what matters most.

A profound lesson from my mother, a surgical nurse, resonates deeply. She shared that during surgery, the essence of humanity shines through because our insides look the same, regardless of our outer appearances. Our differences are only skin deep.

Imagine not being confined to the color of your skin but rather embracing the richness of your identity and the strength of your spirit. We are all interconnected, and it's time to celebrate our diversity without losing sight of our unity.

Let go of self-hate and embrace the beauty within you. Choose to uplift one another, recognizing that we are all part of something greater. Let love and understanding guide your journey, and together, let's rise above!

But what do many poor people do in the hood? They gamble. They blame their plight on racism but then buy scratch-offs, play the lottery, play the numbers, and they play march madness squares. I never understood sports gambling that went on when I was living in the hood. This was always a mystery to me. I used to always see people running around with some papers with some squares on them and I used to wonder what they were doing when I saw them get money. Till this day, I don't know what they are doing, but in the hood, people want money, but many don't want God. Hood people want the blessing without the blesser! Instead of being responsible with the money they get, they want to spend their money however they fancy (on cigarettes, liquor, weed, porn, gambling, etc.) and then want God to help them hit the Power Ball. It seems like there was schizophrenia when I was growing up in the hood. Our minds were not right, we wanted money but had no integrity, we wanted money but had no morality. We wanted to sleep with whoever we wanted to sleep with. Yet, the number one rule of wealth is to have a family so wealthy that it can be perpetuated to the next generation. The homes were so broken, and people were sleeping with whoever they wanted to sleep with; two or three people at the same time. Many women didn't even know who the real father of their child was, but our people wanted more money. We want the government to pour millions and billions more into the community. We want money, but we don't want morality. So, when you come through the door and you get with Jesus, the kingdom is opened to you. And y'all, in God's kingdom is everything you need! In His kingdom is wealth. In His kingdom is real-estate. In His kingdom there's riches. But there are some prerequisites!

Look at Psalms 112:1-2, *"Praise ye the LORD. Blessed is the man that feareth the LORD, That delighteth greatly in his commandments. ² His seed shall be mighty upon the earth: The generation of the upright shall be blessed."*

No more blame game people. God has made provision for us. No more blaming anyone. Learn God's Kingdonomics – that is the Kingdom's Economics, and you will be blessed no matter what.

Chapter 4 | Kingdonomics
Willing & Obedient

People in the hood feel there is no hope. I grew up going to church and by the time the late 1980s hit, the black church was in a rapid decline. The entire nation had gone through a crisis of faith through the PTL Jim Bakker scandal. The black community was losing faith in Christianity and had turned to Afro-centrism and the Nation of Islam for any real hope of social and economic change. During this time, the black church was losing 200 black man a day to Islam. The brand of Christianity I was taught had everything to do with going to Heaven when I died. What I call SIMPLE salvation. I had never been taught the total gospel message or what some call the Full Gospel. Many black Christians at the time had grown disillusioned with the "Pie In the Sky" version of the gospel that most of us had been taught. This concept that Jesus died so that you could go to Heaven and only there would you receive all of luxuries and prosperity was predominately being taught in churches, but no one in my particular denomination was teaching the other part of the Gospel. Hear what Jesus said when He first used the word "gospel":

Luke 4:18-19 (KJV) "^{18} The Spirit of the Lord is upon me, because he hath anointed me to preach the gospel to the poor; he hath sent me to heal the brokenhearted, to preach deliverance to the captives, and recovering of sight to the blind, to set at liberty them that are bruised, ^{19} To preach the acceptable year of the Lord."

In the first message, He first stated that the gospel is for the poor. Let me translate that for urban America, "the hood." He said I have been anointed to preach the gospel to "the hood." The only hope for the hood is Jesus. The only hope for change in the hood is the full gospel. What is good news to the poor? You don't have to be poor anymore. The government has been preaching a pseudo-gospel to the poor: "We will take care of your financial needs". But it was a lie. The hood is worst-off because of these programs, but Jesus came to preach the "almost-too-good-to-be-true news" to the poor that He came to provide abundance.

John 10:10 (KJV) "The thief cometh not, but for to steal, and to kill, and to destroy: I am come that they might have life, and that they might have it more abundantly."

When I got a hold of this truth it began to change everything. There were plenty of new principles I had to learn about money and abundance. But the first thing was that God wanted me to prosper and have abundance.

Let's look at Isaiah 1:19 (KJV) *"^{19} If ye be willing and obedient, ye shall eat the good of the land."*

Do you want to have wealth? What does this mean? This means that even if I'm in the "hood", even if I was raised without a father in the home, even if my parents handed me poverty, and even if I'm on food stamps and government assistance, **IF** I become willing and obedient to God, He would cause me to eat the good of the land. The good of the land means the best in the land available at the time. So, in the 1930s the best car available was a 1934 Ford DeLuxe Roadster. Most cars didn't have air conditioners, and none had automatic windows or CD players, but the

Roadster was the best at that time. This is what was available to a willing and obedient Christian back then. What was the best transportation in Jesus' day? Horses and chariots!

So, I want you to think of the best luxurious car today. Did you know God wants you to have it? This was the first hurdle I had to overcome and maybe the first one for you. Can you wrap your brain around the fact the God wants His children to drive the best, wear the best, and live in the best?

I had a hard time with this, because somewhere it was taught or inferred that people who had the best things were either unsaved or wicked. Out of all the examples of wealthy people in the Bible: Adam, Abraham, Isaac, Jacob, Moses, Joseph, David, Solomon, Esther, Boaz, etc., the preachers against prosperity only emphasized the rich young ruler, or the rich man that went to hell. They emphasized his story and used him as the model for how we should see wealth.

1 Timothy 6:10 (KJV) "For the love of money is the root of all evil: which while some coveted after, they have erred from the faith, and pierced themselves through with many sorrows."

Let us explain this dichotomy. It is the "love" of money that's the root of all evil, not the money. Look at Job. He was rich but didn't love money.

Job 1:1-3 (CEV) "He was a truly good person, who respected God and refused to do evil. ²Job had seven sons and three daughters. ³He owned seven thousand sheep, three thousand camels, five hundred pair of oxen, five hundred donkeys, and a large number of servants. He was the richest person in the East."

Job loved Go, not money. Abraham refused to take money from the king of Sodom; even though he was already rich. This proved that he loved God, not money.

Genesis 14:23 (TLB) "that I will not take so much as a single thread from you, lest you say, 'Abram is rich because of what I gave him!"

We were always taught that if you get too much money that means you will love it, but I have seen more people love money who are poor and didn't have money than those with an abundance of money. When you rob people and beat up old ladies to steal money from their purse, you probably love money. When people sell drugs to their own people for money, even though they know it kills them, they probably love money. When a man will lose his whole paycheck gambling, he probably loves money. When a woman is willing to swing her naked body around a pole or sell her body in prostitution, although she knows it puts her life in danger, she probably loves money. Notice selling drugs, robbing, gambling, and prostitution are all evil, but the root of those activities is the love of money.

God has a remedy for greed and loving money. It's God's way in the kingdom to make sure that no one that gets rich the right way ever starts loving money. The secret is generosity. He commands that we give. This prevents us from ever getting too attached to money, wealth, or material things. God has told me to give tens of thousands of dollars away, to give cars away, and I've even virtually gave a house away. The Lord requires that those in the church, who get rich in His kingdom, stay sober and not be high-minded. Listen to this scripture, which is an admonishment to those that are rich in the church:

1 Timothy 6:17-18 (KJV) "^{17} Charge them that are rich in this world, that they be not highminded, nor trust in uncertain riches, but in the living God, who giveth us richly all things to enjoy; ^{18} That they do good, that they be rich in good works, ready to distribute, willing to communicate."

Here are a few scriptures you must meditate that tells you God wants His people to be rich, to have abundance, and be prosperous. Meditate on these scriptures and get them in your spirit.

Genesis 12:1-2 (KJV) "^{1} Now the LORD had said unto Abram, Get thee out of thy country, and from thy kindred, and from thy father's house, unto a land that I will shew thee: ^{2} And I will make of thee a great nation, and I will bless thee, and make thy name great; and thou shalt be a blessing:"

Genesis 13:2 (KJV) "And Abram was very rich in cattle, in silver, and in gold."

Galatians 3:13-14 (KJV) "^{13} Christ hath redeemed us from the curse of the law, being made a curse for us: for it is written, Cursed is every one that hangeth on a tree: ^{14} That the blessing of Abraham might come on the Gentiles through Jesus Christ; that we might receive the promise of the Spirit through faith."

Psalms 35:27 (KJV) "Let them shout for joy, and be glad, that favour my righteous cause: yea, let them say continually, Let the LORD be magnified, which hath pleasure in the prosperity of his servant."

Proverbs 10:22 (KJV) "The blessing of the LORD, it maketh rich, and he addeth no sorrow with it."

Psalms 112:1-3 (KJV) "1 Praise ye the LORD. Blessed is the man that feareth the LORD, that delighteth greatly in his commandments. 2 His seed shall be mighty upon earth: the generation of the upright shall be blessed. 3 Wealth and riches shall be in his house: and his righteousness endureth for ever."

3 John 1:2 (KJV) "Beloved, I wish above all things that thou mayest prosper and be in health, even as thy soul prospereth."

God wants you blessed. He wants you to be prosperous.

Isaiah 1:19 (KJV) "If ye be willing and obedient, ye shall eat the good of the land:"

Chapter 5 | Kingdonomics

Willing and Obedient= WO?

Do you really want to be obedient? Most people don't associate obedience with blessings, but the scripture says, "If you are willing and obedient, you shall eat the good of the land." The first letters of those two words are 'willing' and 'obedient'. I spell out 'WO!' That's the kind of response I want people to have when they look at my life.

You see, back when I was in the 'hood,' nobody looked at my life and said "WO!" They just had pity on me. But now, 40 years later, they look at my life and say, "WO!" Why? Because I am committed to being willing and obedient. That's the key to experiencing God's blessings.

If you are willing and obedient, do you know what that means? It means you'll drive the best cars, live in the best houses, wear the best clothes, and your kids will get the best education! Autonomy is what hurts us in the hood. When you're growing up without supervision, it's so easy to just look out for number one. But in God's kingdom, it's different.

The Bible says that He'll give you pastors that will feed you and watch over your soul (ref. Jeremiah 3:15). There's no autonomy in the local church. What God is trying to do is connect you with people who are blessed and know what it takes to be blessed, so they can walk you through to the blessing. To do that, you've got to be willing and obedient.

What is the first thing a poor person needs to grow financially and get out of the hood? Food stamps? Welfare? Housing? No! The first thing they need is to learn to be willing and obedient to the Lord. That's the key to experiencing God's best for their lives. So, let me ask YOU. Are you willing to be obedient? If you are, I guarantee you that people are going to look at your life one day and say, "WO!" Are you willing to learn obedience in new areas? I had to learn obedience in three primary areas and these three subjects changed my life forever: Wisdom, Faith, and Love. I call it the "waffle lessons." (Because WFL sounds like the word "waffle."). When a person starts walking in Wisdom, Faith, and Love, everyone around you will begin to say, "WO!"

Now take my mom, she had to work night shift and did what she had to do to make money. My mother hadn't discovered all the principles of prosperity, but she had the first part right: She was willing! Willing to do what she had to do to take care of us and never saw her plot for welfare. She was willing to work hard and never got food stamps. She was willing to take full responsibility for her finances, when she could've taken my dad to court and got child support but never did. My mom was the poster child for welfare in the 1970s: a black, single-mom in the "hood." But she said in herself, "I can do this!" She was willing. If you're a single mom reading this, you better get some grit, some spit, some unction, and some gumption! I don't care what the world tells you. You don't need the government, and you don't need Uncle Sam! If you got God and the breath of life in your lungs, you can make it! Because God said He'll be a father to the fatherless and the husband to the ones that don't have a husband! *(reference Psalm 68:5)*

Which Kingdom Will You Choose?

But poor people, especially African-American poor people, must choose which kingdom they belong to. Because Minister Louis Farrakhan is going to tell you, "this is the year, and this is the century of the black man. This is the time for the black man! The white man had his time, the red man had his time, the yellow man had his time, this is the time for the black man!" Everybody's looking for another way and another kingdom. Even right after the resurrection, Jesus' disciples asked Him about another kingdom, not the kingdom of God. Let's look at the Word:

Acts 1:6 (KJV) "⁶ When they therefore were come together, they asked of him, saying, Lord, wilt thou at this time restore again the kingdom to Israel? Look at verse 3 what did Jesus talk about?"

Acts 1:3 (KJV) "³ To whom also he shewed himself alive after his passion by many infallible proofs, being seen of them forty days, and speaking of the things pertaining to the kingdom of God."

Jesus talked about the kingdom of God, but they wanted to know about the kingdom of "their" people.

We hear these voices in our community all the time: "When are we going to rise up? When are we going to come together?" I spent a few years during college being Afrocentric, chasing what I thought was my identity down a rabbit hole, and found it to be futile. I'm not going to waste my life trying to figure out when our people, who can't get together on ANYTHING, are going to rise up. WHY? Because I'm a part of another kingdom!

I'm not a part of the Nation of Islam, and I'm not a part of the Nation of Black Nationalists. I am a part of a Holy Nation, a royal priesthood, a peculiar people—and that's what everyone who is poor and living in the "hood" needs. They need somebody to bring them Christ and someone to bring them the real Kingdom.

Y'all, I know people who have been chasing that black power rabbit for 50 years. They don't have any properties, they don't own a car, and they haven't gotten anywhere in life. But years ago, I pledged to Jesus under God that I would serve Him with all of my mind and all of my heart and all of my soul—with all of my life—everything going into one direction: the Kingdom of God!

Notice how Jesus responded to His disciple when they were talking about their ethnocentric kingdom:

Acts 1:7 (KJV) "And he said unto them, It is not for you to know the times or the seasons, which the father hath put in his own power."

But then he flipped the conversation in verse 8:

Acts 1:8 "But ye shall receive power, after that the Holy Ghost is come upon you: and ye shall be witnesses unto me both in Jerusalem, and in all Judaea, and in Samaria, and unto the uttermost part of the earth."

Jesus was saying, "My kingdom trumps all other kingdoms." That's why they call Jesus the King of Kings and the Lord of Lords. He told them, "Don't worry about those other little kingdoms, but get into My kingdom, and I'm going to give you some power—and My power is going to affect Jerusalem, Judea, Samaria, and all the other parts of the world."

Which kingdom do you want to be in?

In the "hood" and in every corner of this world, people are searching for hope—for a way out of poverty and despair. People chase after false promises of power and prosperity, yet these earthly kingdoms can never satisfy the deepest longings of the human soul. There is a plethora of doors out of the "hood": education, sports, singing, acting, selling drugs, entrepreneurship, grant writing, "gaming the system," gambling, stripping, etc. But the ultimate truth is that Jesus is the door and the way to the Kingdom of God. Through Him, we receive the power of the Holy Spirit to be His witnesses—to bring the gospel of salvation to Jerusalem, Judea, Samaria, and to the ends of the earth. The word "salvation" in the Greek means: prosperity, health, and eternal life in Heaven. So, true prosperity can only be achieved through Jesus.

It matters not the color of our skin or our economic status because Jesus came to save all people. So let us not be afraid to enter the "hood" and share the transformative love of Christ. For when a lost soul encounters the risen Lord, anything is possible. We have seen nappy-headed boys and girls; black, white, and Hispanic—all have had their lives turned around by the miracle-working power of God.

So let us fix our eyes on Him, pledging our whole hearts, minds, and souls to serve the King of Kings. He is the answer the people in the "hood" need and the only true path out of poverty, darkness, and into the glorious light of salvation. In the hood, there are a lot of kingdoms and a lot of doors out of the hood. There are people promising a way out of poverty when you're in the hood. But you've got to choose which door you're going through. Jesus said, "I am the door"—that's John 10:9. He was the door to the Kingdom.

Do you know I'm not scared of the hood? I go to the hood as often as I can, and I share Jesus. That's all they need. I share my testimony. There's nothing more amazing than to take a little nappy-headed Black boy that nobody thought had a chance, get him saved, get him born again, and watch God take him through the pathways, the vastitude, dangers seen and unseen, and produce something out of his life. Same thing with a little girl. You don't have to be black—you can be white, you can be Hispanic, you can be in the hood living in poverty. But the answer is Jesus.

Say this out loud: The answer is Jesus! His Kingdom trumps all other kingdoms. Look at Psalm 112:3–4:

"³ Wealth and riches shall be in his house: and his righteousness endureth for ever. ⁴ Unto the upright there ariseth light in the darkness..."

When you get saved in the hood, the light comes on you. It doesn't wait for you to move; it rises on you while you're still in the hood. That light makes you an anomaly. It makes you a misfit. It makes you an outsider. But not for long, because in a minute, you're going to be moving out of the hood into the good.

The danger is this: too many people give up on the process too early. They don't realize that transformation is already in motion. They're walking in the light even while surrounded by darkness. That's why the Bible said, "Do not be weary in well doing, for in due season you'll reap if you faint not." Wealth and riches—who doesn't want that? This is the formula right here. It tells you. Let's go back over the steps:

1. You got to choose which kingdom you're going to put all your eggs in that basket. You know there are people that come to church and argue in their mind

with the theology of the pastor. "We not woke enough," they say. "They don't know the knowledge of self," they say. You got to choose which kingdom you want.

2. After you choose the kingdom, if Jesus is the kingdom, after you choose Jesus, you walk through the door. Then you got to learn kingdom rules. See, there are hood rules, and there are kingdom rules. Hood rules is when I see a hundred dollars hanging out of your back pocket and it falls on the ground, and I wait till you leave. We call that, "We just caught you slipping." That's hood rules.

Hood rules is in the grocery store: you give them twenty, but they give you change for a fifty. Hood rules say that's a blessing—"God must have knew I needed some extra money for my light bill." But the kingdom rules say, "No sir, no ma'am, you gave me too much change." Two claps on that. That's the people who just got a house because they learned the difference between the hood rules and the kingdom rules.

You got to start learning the ways of God. And the beginning of wisdom, which are the ways of God, is the fear of the Lord. There are all kinds of rules.

You know there's hood sex... I'm going to look down. Hood sex be good for the moment, Jack. You can do anything in hood sex because there are no rules. Until it's time to go to the clinic. It's all fun and games until someone gets pregnant. You have got to learn the difference in the kingdom.

So, when you step into the kingdom, you hood people that think you know everything have to humble yourself and get stupid. "I don't know nothing, Pastor" or "Whatever you tell me I need to do, that's what I'm going to do, because I want the blessing." Don't come in here interjecting, don't come in here giving advice! Don't come in here trying to say what you know! You don't know nothing in the kingdom! You got to learn the rules of the kingdom. That's the problem with black folks, they say they want to come to the kingdom with the same stuff they was doing in the hood and it won't work! So, every time you correct someone, they say, "They condemning me!" And every time you sit someone down, they say, "They wouldn't let me do anything." No, you got to learn. Come on, somebody. You're coming to the family of God as a baby. You might have been a full-grown man in the hood, but you come in here as a babe, and babies don't know nothing but how to eat and how to poop. Cry, sleep, eat, and poop. But if you're already dedicated to moving from the hood to eating the good, you ought to make some noise right now. You ought to let the devil know. You got to make enough noise that the devil understands. Them demons that had you bound, and them demons that used to come to your house on Friday night at 10 o'clock, they back up because they know this time she ain't playin'! If I could ever get you excited about the process—if I could ever get you excited that if you just humble yourself and get willing and obedient, you would have the good of the land.

See, in the world, it's how high you go, but in the kingdom, it's how low you go. In the world, it's how much you get, but in the kingdom, it's how much you give. In the world, it's how much you hate, but in the kingdom, it's how much you love. You got to learn.

I don't miss the hood. I don't miss the hood rules. I don't miss the hood sex. God gave me a good woman, and good

God Almighty, it keeps getting better and better. In the hood, the sex gets worser and worse, but I'll tell you one thing: give your body over to God, a living sacrifice, holy and acceptable unto Him, and let Him bring you the man or woman He wants you to have.

If I had two people who'd rise up with excitement about coming out of the hood, I'd celebrate right now. I know what it's like. I know what it's like to hear gunshots at night. I know what it's like not to have enough food. I know what it's like to eat government cheese. I know what it's like. But when God blesses you, He is going to make you rich. The blessing of the Lord makes you rich and adds no sorrow.

How many people will be honest enough to say, "I've been trying to work the kingdom like I work the hood"? How many will say, "I need to learn. I need to learn the kingdom. I need to learn the ways of the kingdom"?

Are you ready to be blessed? Can you stand to be blessed?

Chapter 6 | Kingdonomics
What is Kingdomnomics?

From the time I was a little boy, I heard various forms of the word *Economics*. It always centered around whoever was the President of the United States at the time—Reaganomics, Clintonomics, and most currently, Bidenomics. However, I coined a term called *Kingdonomics* as I was preaching a series by the same name. But what is *Kingdonomics*? If Reaganomics was President Ronald Reagan's economic plan for America, then Kingdonomics is God's economic plan for His people.

Dr. Gabriel Rogers, from Kingdom Christian Church, preached a series years ago called "Switching Kingdoms." This message compelled the believer to switch over from the kingdom of the world's mindset to the Kingdom of God's mindset. Most Christians are still operating with the knowledge that came from the kingdom of the world, especially regarding financing. There are so many misconceptions that Christians have about money. I had many misconceptions until God straightened me out, and as my brother Dr. Rogers taught, I switched kingdoms.

One misconception I had was about work. I thought that the Bible taught that *work* was the result of the curse. I found out this was not true. Secondly, I found out that God wanted us to live in abundance, not lack. Thirdly, I learned God wanted us to rule and reign as kings. Last, all this was lost when man and woman sinned and activated the cursed toil-sweat system.

Genesis 2:2 (KJV) "2 And on the seventh day God ended his work which he had made; and he rested on the seventh day from all his work which he had made."

The Hebrew word "work" means:

AV (167) - work 129, business 12, workmen + h6213 7, workmanship 5, goods 2, cattle 1, stuff 1, thing 1, misc. 9;

occupation, work, business occupation, business property work (something done or made) workmanship service, use public business.

So work isn't a bad thing. God was the first one on the planet that worked. Part of God's work was creating wealth and abundance for His finest creation: man. So many people think badly of God's people when they have wealth or abundance. "Christians shouldn't have money. Christians shouldn't own private jets." But I started asking the questions: Where did abundance come from? God created abundance. Who did He make it for? Satan and his people? No. But most people don't say anything about a devil-worshipping rock band having a private jet. Nobody says anything about the huge mansion some NBA star lives in. Everybody thinks it's great if some rapper has 15 to 20 cars in his oversized garage. But God didn't create wealth and abundance for all of the secular people. He created it and provided it for His people. Read this scripture.

Psalms 24:1 (KJV) "¹ The earth is the LORD's, and the fulness thereof; the world, and they that dwell therein."

Everything in the earth belongs to God—all the gold, the silver, the oil, the gas, everything. Yet Satan has tricked man into handing it over to him and his people. This is why when Satan tempted Jesus, he said this:

Luke 4:5–6 (AMP) "⁵ Then the devil took Him up to a high mountain and showed Him all the kingdoms of the habitable world in a moment of time [in the twinkling of an eye]. ⁶ And he said to Him, To You I will give all this power and authority and their glory (all their magnificence, excellence, preeminence, dignity, and grace), for it has been turned over to me, and I give it to whomever I will."

Who turned it over to Satan? Was it God? No. God gave it to His man—remember?

Genesis 1:26 (AMP) "²⁶ God said, Let Us [Father, Son, and Holy Spirit] make mankind in Our image, after Our likeness, and let them have complete authority over the fish of the sea, the birds of the air, the [tame] beasts, and over all of the earth, and over everything that creeps upon the earth."

So, how did Satan get the kingdoms of the world and all the glory? Here is the answer: God gave it to Adam, and then Adam gave it to Satan through his obedience to him instead of God.

Of course, the New Testament hadn't been written, but this principle was already in the earth:

Romans 6:16 (KJV) "Know ye not, that to whom ye yield yourselves servants to obey, his servants ye are to whom ye obey; whether of sin unto death, or of obedience unto righteousness?"

Adam yielded to the Devil, and then he forfeited everything to him and became his slave. Now THIS IS BIG. You have to understand this to understand that God wants His people to prosper.

Think of this: Let's say I give John my car to use, and he has my only set of keys. I tell John the car is for you to drive as long as you want, but don't give it to Jim. Jim comes along and somehow tricks John into giving him the keys, and Jim takes the car.

Who has possession of the car? Jim.

Who has control of the car? Jim.

Who did I want to have and control the car? John.

But now Jim has it.

So now, since Jim has had the car for so long, when John comes back and gets the keys back, people think somehow John is wrong. They act like John is the criminal, yet the car was meant for John all along.

Jay-Z owns two private jets given to him as gifts from Beyoncé, his wife. But if a pastor's wife has enough money to give him one jet, Inside Edition, TMZ, The New York Times, and every other news outlet would report on it as extreme excess and misappropriation of religious money.

(Admittedly, there has been fraud by some people claiming to be with the Church and claiming to be "so-called pastors.") But in an alternate universe where Adam had obeyed God, it would be out of place for the Devil's people to have wealth and private jets—and normal for God's people to have it.

If you can understand this, you will know and believe that God absolutely and unequivocally wants you, as a Christian believer, to be wealthy. This was the beginning for me changing my mind and changing my income. I had to understand that God wanted me in abundance and not lack.

Now, there are fellow pastors that preach against what I'm teaching and call it the "prosperity gospel." They even made a movie about this and put it on Netflix. But some of the same people who criticize prosperity are richer than some of us who preach it. No defamation to anyone, and I only call names because these guys have come out so publicly and harshly against Christians having wealth. The net worth of one of the greatest prosperity opponents, as of the time of this writing, is estimated at $10 to $30 million and he lives in a home worth $1.5 million. Another opponent of our message has a net worth between $6 million and $12 million. I have no problem with these ministers having this type of income. Most of it came from the sale of their own books. However, these men seem to have a problem with the rest of us having wealth.

Settle this forever: **GOD WANTS HIS PEOPLE TO HAVE WEALTH, NOT THE DEVIL'S PEOPLE.**

The third lesson I learned about money and prosperity was that God wanted us to rule as kings in life. I have never met a poor king. I have never heard of a king on food stamps. Have you?

Listen to the Word of God:

Romans 5:17 (AMP) "For if because of one man's trespass (lapse, offense) death reigned through that one, much more surely will those who receive [God's] overflowing grace (unmerited favor) and the free gift of righteousness [putting them into right standing with Himself] reign as kings in life through the one Man Jesus Christ (the Messiah, the Anointed One)."

Christians are to reign as kings. Period. While Jesus lived on earth, we don't see Him begging like a pauper. We see Him ruling as a king. No food to feed the 5,000? Did He beg Herod for government assistance? Did He go and ask unbelievers for money to help Him feed His followers? No. He took up an offering from a little boy, spoke to it, and it multiplied.

Kings rule by decrees. So do kings work? Yes. Do they toil and sweat? No. Their work is ruling, and they rule mainly by decreeing. This is how God wants the believer to live.

I learned this years ago when I was trying out the Word of Faith teachings. I was learning about faith—not from all of the men who may have perverted it over the years—but from the father himself, Kenneth Hagin. I was listening to his tapes and messages on faith. He had been diagnosed with three different heart conditions and blood diseases.

Doctors said he wouldn't live past his 17th birthday. But he found Mark 11:23–24 in the Bible, believed it, and was miraculously healed. I took Mark 11:23–24 which said:

Mark 11:23–24 (KJV) "[23] For verily I say unto you, That whosoever shall say unto this mountain, Be thou removed, and be thou cast into the sea; and shall not doubt in his heart, but shall believe that those things which he saith shall come to pass; he shall have whatsoever he saith. [24] Therefore I say unto you, What things soever ye desire, when ye pray, believe that ye receive them, and ye shall have them."

And I tested it for myself. I said, "God, if this works I will preach this all over America. If it doesn't work, I will tell everyone that God's Word pertaining to faith stuff is a lie, and it doesn't work!" I needed $1,000 in a few days or else my only car would be repossessed by the finance company.

Here is the very interesting backstory. Tyler Perry (who we currently do not endorse) was in Houston performing his first national play: *"Lord I Know I've Been Changed."* At this time, he would do altar calls at the end of his plays and called on ministers in the city to help lead people to Christ. This was when Tyler Perry first started—isn't that amazing?

I was one of the many ministers he chose to do this. We could go to the shows as many times as we wanted and bring our family as well.

So it was on Sunday, May 30, 1999, that I tried the Mark 11:23–24 Scripture. I remember it because it was the last Sunday of Tyler Perry's play being in Houston, TX. I had three to four hours between our morning service and the 3 p.m. curtain call. I decided that I would go into my bedroom and not come out until I had gotten in faith for the $1,000 I needed for my vehicle. So I took out my Bible and turned to the passage:

Mark 11:23–24 (KJV) "For verily I say unto you, That whosoever shall say unto this mountain, Be thou removed, and be thou cast into the sea; and shall not doubt in his heart, but shall believe that those things which he saith shall come to pass; he shall have whatsoever he saith. Therefore I say unto you, What things soever ye desire, when ye pray, believe that ye receive them, and ye shall have them."

I read this verse out loud and I prayed. I said, "Lord, I believe Your Word, and I will not leave this room until I have met the conditions of faith. Furthermore, I will not tell anyone about this $1,000 need, so that when You supply the money, You will get all the glory. In Jesus' name." Then I got up from kneeling and proceeded to walk out of the bedroom. But as soon as I got up, I immediately started worrying and doubting in my mind. The devil said over and over, "What are you going to do now? What are you going to do now? That's crazy stuff. It doesn't work. You're not going to get the money, and then your car is going to get repoed. You better ask your mama for the money. That's the only vehicle you and your wife have. How are you going to get to work? Blah, blah, blah."

So what did I do? I turned around, got back on my knees, and prayed the same thing all over again. I ended it the same way: "...furthermore I will not tell anyone about this $1,000 need, so that when You supply the money You will get all the glory. In Jesus' name." I got up to open the door thinking I was done, but as soon as I got up, the devil started in again: "Look at you doing that dumb faith stuff. That stuff doesn't work. You still don't have the money. You might as well borrow the money from your father-in-law and pay it back. What are you going to do now? What are you going to do now?" So I turned around and got back down on my knees. You may ask, why did you keep doing that? Because if I had left out of that room with all that doubt in my mind, I wouldn't have met the conditions of Mark 11:23–24, and I would have broken my promise to God that I would stay in the room until I had met the conditions of faith.

So I did this over and over for about an hour. Then I heard the Lord say, *"Read verse 24 again…"* and I did. All of a sudden something stood out to me:

"²⁴ Therefore I say unto you, What things soever ye desire, when ye pray, **believe that ye receive them**, and ye shall have them."

The Lord asked me, *"Rondy, when should you believe you received the $1,000?"* I said, "According to this verse, when I pray I should believe I received." The Lord asked me, *"Then how would you act if someone knocked on your door right now and gave you $1,000 cash? How would you act? What would you do?"*

Right then—I got it! I saw where I was missing faith and how the devil was able to immediately get me into doubt after I prayed. I really hadn't believed that I received.

So I got down on my knees one more time. I went through my prayer and scripture confession again, but this time when I ended my prayer I said, *"...and I believe I receive the $1,000 right now in Jesus' name."* Then I got off of my knees and acted like I already had the money. I started shouting and dancing and leaping and beating on the dresser with joy and elation. My wife came in the room and asked me what I was doing. I told her that I was happy because we had received the $1,000 we needed. Then she got excited and asked where the money was. When I told her I had received it by faith, I could see the disappointment in her face but it didn't bother me. I was in faith. No more doubt. I walked out of that room and went to the Tyler Perry play. It was around 3 p.m. in the afternoon on Sunday, May 30, 1999. One of the associate preachers from the church I was serving at picked me up, and we went and prayed with those accepting Christ at the Tyler Perry play. Then we left there and went to another evening church service.

After the sermon, the pastor of the church did an altar call for those having financial problems. Did I go forward? What do you think? Do you think I should've gone forward? I may have gone forward, and then someone in the audience with $1,000 might have seen me and felt sorry for me and given me the money, right? Well, the answer is no. I didn't go forward. Why? Because I didn't have any financial problems. I had settled that in the room before I left the house. I believed I received the money—remember? That's just as good as someone writing me a $1,000 check. Usually, it takes time for a check to clear once I put it in the bank. So the fact that I wasn't able to use the $1,000 yet didn't matter. Any day now I would have access to the money. This is the same way it works in faith. The moment you believe you received, then you have it in the spirit—it just hasn't posted to your physical account yet.

Instead of going up to get prayed for, the pastor called me up to pray for a young man having financial problems. This was also an act of faith. Then the Lord told me to do something that I will never forget: *"Give that young man $10."* All I had in the whole entire world was $20, and God told me to give half of my treasure to this young man.

This was a very important principle: *If you have a need, sow a seed!* So I gave $10 to the young man. Now what happens seven days later is almost unbelievable...

It was Saturday, June 5, 1999, at approximately 3 p.m. I was attending a church picnic at Clinton Park, 2000 Mississippi Street in East Houston, and a man walked up to me and gave me an envelope. He said he had a message from God for me: *"Never let money come between you and God ever again."* I said, "Thank you, brother," and didn't think much of it. He told me to keep the envelope safe and warned me not to lose it. When I got home, I opened the envelope and discovered ten crispy $100 bills.

Now in 1999, a Black man giving another Black man $1,000 was unheard of. As I write this book 26 years later, this would still be considered miraculous—and it all happened in the 'hood. The median income in the area at the time was $19,000. It was a poor area. So how did this prosperous moment happen? By grace through my faith.

I paid my car note and avoided the repossession of my 1988 Lincoln Town Car, which I had bought from the Mel Farr Ford dealership.

Chapter 7 | Kingdonomics
Faith or Foolishness?

So yes, during these first stages of learning Kingdonomics, the Lord was teaching me faith. I had other instances like the $1,000 account in the envelope. While foolishly quitting my job to go into full-time ministry, I believed God for a place to stay after we got evicted. The same manager that evicted us from our tiny one-bedroom apartment called us after the eviction and offered us a brand-new two-bedroom apartment with ceiling fans. (Ceiling fans were a big luxury in the '90s.) If that's not enough of a miracle, it was rent-free for two years.

God did things over and over like that to teach me faith.

The next thing He began to teach me was wisdom. Here's what I've learned about faith: faith can get you a miracle, but wisdom prevents you from needing one. Do you remember the $1,000? I needed it to prevent my vehicle from being repossessed. Do you know that months later, that same car still got repossessed? Why? Because I didn't have wisdom when it came to finances.

I've also noticed this in the Faith camp, churches like mine that people call Word of Faith. Some of us are just downright kooky and weird. Instead of applying wisdom, we try to apply faith to foolishness. For instance, during this time in my life, I had a wife and a child, and I had quit a great-paying job to go into full-time ministry. So every day, I would wake up and believe God for food to eat for myself, my wife, and my child. This was insane. The Bible clearly says, *"If you don't work, you don't eat."* (reference 2 Thessalonians 3:10) To eat, a man needs to work. So instead of using the wisdom of the Word and getting my old job back, I was out on the street trying to sell my own preaching cassettes to get money to eat. God finally got through to me, and I went back to work. But I put my wife and family through unnecessary hardship.

So, what did I have to learn? The most important thing. Do you know what the Bible says is the most important thing? Is it money, faith, prayer? And yes—all of these are very important. Let's find out what the Bible says.

Proverbs 4:7-10 (TLB) "⁷ Getting wisdom is the most important thing you can do! And with your wisdom, develop common sense and good judgment. ⁸⁻⁹ If you exalt wisdom, she will exalt you. Hold her fast, and she will lead you to great honor; she will place a beautiful crown upon your head. ¹⁰ My son, listen to me and do as I say, and you will have a long, good life."

Getting wisdom is the most important thing you can do. Yes—if you are going to move into wealth, you have to move into wisdom first. Most people who don't have money don't live by wisdom. Honestly, I have never met a poor person who had financial wisdom. The first thing I discovered about God is that He doesn't rule the universe by feelings, or by committee, or by daily illogical decisions. No. God rules the universe by laws. He doesn't decide daily what time the sun will come up or whether gravity will work today. There are laws that govern the solar system. There is a law of gravity. So wisdom is the set of laws that govern success, health, and wealth.

In 2003, I found some discarded tapes that changed my life forever. They were called *101 Wisdom Keys*. I had never heard any of the things that were being discussed on these tapes. Don't get me wrong—my mother and grandparents had taught me basic wisdom, or what most people call "common sense." But I had never had life explained to me like this. It was like pouring water into a person's mouth who's been stranded in the Sahara Desert for three months, with parched and cracked lips and a dry throat.

I drank those wisdom keys up like they were life-saving water—because they were. Wisdom keys changed my life forever.

The Bible has a lot to say about money, wealth, debt, loaning money, earning money, starting businesses, giving money, sowing money, investing money, saving money, loving money, and the uncertainty of money. This is God's financial wisdom. What I've discovered over the years is that most Christians want God's money miracles, but not

God's money wisdom. Let me share one of the wisdom keys that changed the way I handle money:

Debt is the proof of greed. There are three categories of financial status:

1. The Haves
2. The Have-Nots
3. The Have-Not-Yet-Paid-for-What-They-Have

People go into debt because they want something they can't afford. People should wait and save up for large purchases. Most items can be planned for and bought with cash instead of making interest payments. You should limit debt and try not to have any if possible. The Bible says:

Romans 13:8 (KJV) "Owe no man any thing, but to love one another: for he that loveth another hath fulfilled the law."

Proverbs 22:7 (NIV) "The rich rule over the poor, and the borrower is slave to the lender."

When my wife and I learned this, we went in reverse and began to apply it—it turned us around financially. First of all, we made a list of all debts. Not just the debts we owed to companies but also the debts we owed to people: our parents, our family members, our friends, etc. We listed every debt and paid every penny back. It was easier than we thought. We would make payments as low as $10 a month or $7 every two weeks. I set them up with my bank account to mail them out automatically. (Most people know to do this with companies, but you can also do this with people too.) It was amazing how quickly you can pay debts back when you do it consistently. Some companies cut a deal with us and greatly reduced the debt. Family members also did this when they saw we were honoring our word and making payments. Many people said, *"Hey, you paid back $150 of the $300 you owe us. We are very impressed with your integrity—we don't need the money, so we'll mark this paid. You don't have to send any more payments."* Wow. God gave us favor when we started living by His financial wisdom keys. Listen to what the Bible says about borrowing and not repaying:

Psalms 37:21 (NIV) "The wicked borrow and do not repay, but the righteous give generously;"

So I was a saved, Holy Ghost-filled, tongue-talking preacher who got scores of people saved and healed. Yet, the Bible calls me "wicked" in my financial dealings. You know, most Christians who are financially in need are "wicked" financially. Ask them if they have debts they haven't paid—and 10 out of 10 times, you'll find that they do. Do you see it? This one piece of wisdom changed everything.

Debt is a curse, and it will curse your ability to get ahead financially. If you borrow money, you must pay it back. You want to prosper and get God's financial blessings? Pay back the money you owe—to people and companies.

Secondly, after we began paying the debts off, we had to change our habit of borrowing money. Do you remember the lyrics to the *Good Times* theme song? *"Easy credit rip-offs...good times."* We cloak borrowing money with terms like financing or buying on credit. But if you're really undoing your finances—or un-financing. You haven't truly purchased anything until you've paid the last payment. Miss three payments and see if you really own what you purchased—they will repo it or foreclose on it.

I remember being saved, sanctified, and filing bankruptcy because I couldn't pay my creditors. I was getting payday loans. I was pawning jewelry and borrowing money against it. I had a bad habit of borrowing money. It was hard, but my wife and I got into agreement and we stopped borrowing and using credit. If we didn't have the money, we would save for it or believe for it, but we wouldn't borrow it.

We began buying all of our cars with cash. We refused to *finance* furniture and appliances. We refused credit cards that were offered, and it was like a miracle—God started doing things supernaturally. We started getting things given to us. Major appliances worth thousands of dollars were given to us for free. I received two gently used Mercedes-Benz cars—given to us for free. This one financial wisdom key changed everything. I'll be sharing more of these wisdom keys in the following volumes of *Kingdonomics*. This is why the Bible says:

Proverbs 4:7 (TLB) "⁷ Getting wisdom is the most important thing you can do!"

(Go to the appendix at the end of this book. List your debts, pray over them, and begin paying them back.)

Prosperity Scripture Confessions

Psalms 128:2 - For I shall eat the labour of thine hands: happy shalt thou be, and it shall be well with me.

2 Corinthians 9:8 - And God is able to make all grace abound toward me; that I, always having all sufficiency in all things, may abound to every good work:

Psalms 1:3 - And I shall be like a tree planted by the rivers of water, that bringeth forth my fruit in my season; my leaf also shall not wither; and whatsoever I doeth shall prosper.

2 Corinthians 8:9 - For I know the grace of our Lord Jesus Christ, that, though he was rich, yet for our sakes he became poor, that we through his poverty might be rich.

Proverbs 28:25 - He that is of a proud heart stirreth up strife: but he that putteth his trust in the LORD shall be made fat.

Deuteronomy 28:13 – I am the head and not the tail; I am above only and not beneath!

Deuteronomy 6:11 – God is giving me houses filled with all kinds of good things I did not provide! He is giving me wells I did not dig and vineyards I did not plant.

Deuteronomy 8:18 – God has given me the ability to produce wealth and to establish His covenant on the earth!

Deuteronomy 1:11 – I thank God for increasing me a thousand times and blessing me as He promised!

Genesis 26:12 – I planted seed and in the same year reaped a hundredfold because the Lord has blessed me!

Psalm 5:12 – I have received the righteousness of Christ! The favor of God surrounds me like a shield!

Psalm 34:9 – I respect the Lord and lack nothing!

Psalm 112:3 – Wealth and riches are in my house!

Proverbs 3:9-10 – I honor the LORD with my possessions and with the first fruits of all my increase; so my barns will be filled with plenty and my vats will overflow with new wine!

Proverbs 10:22 – The blessing of the Lord is on me and it brings wealth with no sorrow!

Proverbs 21:21 – Because I pursue righteousness and love, I've found life, prosperity, and honor!

Malachi 3:10-12 – I bring all the tithes into the storehouse so that there is sustenance in God's house. I try the Lord in this knowing that He will open the windows of Heaven and pour me out a blessing I don't have room enough to contain! God rebukes the devourer for my sake, so that he will not destroy the fruit of my ground or cause my vines to fail in bringing forth fruit! All nations will call me blessed!

Matthew 6:33 – I seek first the kingdom of God and His righteousness, and all the things I need and desire shall be added unto me!

Mark 4:8 – I sow in good ground and yield fruit that springs up and increases, bringing me thirty, sixty, and a hundredfold increase.

Luke 6:38 – I give and it is given back to me – good measure, pressed down, shaken together, and running over, others will give into my bosom! For with the same measure that I use, it will be measured back to me!

Philippians 4:19 – God shall supply all my needs according to His riches in glory by Christ Jesus!

Galatians 3:14 – Jesus has redeemed me and opened the door so that the blessing of Abraham can come to me! By faith I receive the promise of His Spirit!

Galatians 6:7 – I am not deceived because I know that God is not mocked – whatsoever a man sows, that will he also reap!

2 Corinthians 9:6-8 – I know that he who sows sparingly will also reap sparingly, and he who sows bountifully will also reap bountifully. So I give with purpose – not grudgingly or of necessity because I know that God loves a cheerful giver. God is able to make all grace abound toward me so that I will have all sufficiency – always and in all things – and enough abundance for every good work He puts on my heart.

3 John 1:2 – I will prosper in all things and be in health, just as my soul – which is my mind, will, and emotions – prospers!

Appendix

Why We Believe in Prosperity

So many have taught against this theme of prosperity. They call it the "prosperity gospel." They call us "prosperity preachers." I am a prosperity preacher. I'm guilty as charged. So, I want to explain this biblically. When God put Adam in the Garden, He stated His will for man and all mankind.

Genesis 1:26-30 (KJV) "²⁶ And God said, Let us make man in our image, after our likeness: and let them have dominion over the fish of the sea, and over the fowl of the air, and over the cattle, and over all the earth, and over every creeping thing that creepeth upon the earth. ²⁷ So God created man in his own image, in the image of God created he him; male and female created he them. ²⁸ And God blessed them, and

God said unto them, Be fruitful, and multiply, and replenish the earth, and subdue it: and have dominion over the fish of the sea, and over the fowl of the air, and over every living thing that moveth upon the earth. ²⁹ And God said, Behold, I have given you every herb bearing seed, which is upon the face of all the earth, and every tree, in the which is the fruit of a tree yielding seed; to you it shall be for meat. ³⁰ And to every beast of the earth, and to every fowl of the air, and to every thing that creepeth upon the earth, wherein there is life, I have given every green herb for meat: and it was so."

Here is my first question: Who owned everything in the earth? To whom did it belong? Some would say it belongs to God, but God gave it to Adam.

Proof 1:

Psalms 115:16 (AMP) "16 The heavens are the Lord's heavens, but the earth has He given to the children of men."

He gave the earth to men. The first man was Adam. So it was God's will for His children to have the wealth of the earth. Read it again: *It is God's will for His children to have the wealth of the earth.* Listen to what He placed in the Garden.

Genesis 2:10-12 (KJV) "¹⁰ And a river went out of Eden to water the garden; and from thence it was parted, and became into four heads. ¹¹ The name of the first is Pison: that is it which compasseth the whole land of Havilah, where there is gold; ¹² And the gold of that land is good: there is bdellium and the onyx stone."

Anyone reading the Bible who is a Christian can clearly see that God wanted His people to be rich and to have gold and precious stones. This is called *wealth*. So let's establish—it was not against God's will for Adam to have gold. He owned all of the lumber.

There is a man in the United States named Archie "Red" Emerson who is worth $6 billion because he owns 2.4 million acres of West Coast timberland, also known as lumber (trees). But Adam owned all the lumber (trees) on earth, which is 126 billion acres. So by present-day standards, Adam would have been worth $315 trillion in lumber alone. Let me ask you—was Adam the richest man on earth or the poorest man on earth before the fall?

We must resolve that God wanted us to have plenty of wealth. I know this is hard for many Christians because we've been taught and trained that to be humble, we must be poor. This is not a biblical teaching. It actually comes from false religion. Buddhist monks take a vow of poverty. Orthodox Catholicism, which is a mixture of Christianity and paganism, also takes a vow of poverty. But no one in the Bible was told to take a vow of poverty.

Find one scripture that shows God's people are supposed to be poor—you can't. So Adam was supposed to be prosperous. When Adam disobeyed God, he forfeited all of his wealth to the devil. This is what Satan was referring to when he tempted Jesus:

*Luke 4:5-6 (KJV) "⁵ And the devil, taking him up into an high mountain, shewed unto him all the kingdoms of the world in a moment of time. ⁶ And the devil said unto him, All this power will I give thee, and the glory of them: **for that is delivered unto me**; and to whomsoever I will I give it."*

Here is the same verse in the Amplified Translation:

Luke 4:5-6 (AMP) "⁵ Then the devil took Him up to a high mountain and showed Him all the kingdoms of the habitable world in a moment of time [in the twinkling of an eye]. ⁶ And he said to Him, To You I will give all this power and authority and their glory (all their magnificence, excellence, preeminence, dignity, and grace), **for it has been turned over to me,** *and I give it to whomever I will."*

Who gave the wealth of the world to Satan? Who turned it over to him? Adam did—not God. God gave it to Adam, and then Satan tricked Adam into turning it over to him. Now Jesus, who is called the "last Adam" in the Scriptures, came to earth:

1 Corinthians 15:45 (AMP) "Thus it is written, The first man Adam became a living being (an individual personality); the last Adam (Christ) became a life-giving Spirit [restoring the dead to life]."

What did He come to do? He tells us...

Luke 19:10 (KJV) "For the Son of man is come to seek and to save **that** *which was lost."*

Notice He didn't say He came to "save those who were lost." He said He came to save *"that"* which was lost.

Of course, it includes people who were lost—but also everything that was lost when Adam sinned. One of those things was *prosperity.* So since the fall, God has been looking for faithful men. You will see that every man after Adam who was righteous—God prospered him. Every man

He finds that's faithful, He causes him to prosper. Take Noah...

Genesis 6:8-9 (KJV) "⁸ But Noah found grace in the eyes of the LORD. ⁹ These are the generations of Noah: Noah was a just man and perfect in his generations, and Noah walked with God."

So, God tells Noah to build an expensive Ark. Let me ask you, do you think Noah is poor? Listen to the dimensions of the Ark.

Genesis 6:14-16 (NLT) "¹⁴ Build a large boat from cypress wood and waterproof it with tar, inside and out. Then construct decks and stalls throughout its interior. ¹⁵ Make the boat 450 feet long, 75 feet wide, and 45 feet high. ¹⁶ Leave an 18-inch opening below the roof all the way around the boat. Put the door on the side, and build three decks inside the boat—lower, middle, and upper."

I recently visited the replica of the Ark in Kentucky, where I met the man who built it. He personally told me it cost $100 million to build the replica, which didn't even include everything Noah would have needed.

The Ark was breathtaking. Noah had to have a wealth of resources to complete it.

Proof #2:

Noah had to have wealth during his time to quit whatever his livelihood was and dedicate the rest of his life and his sons' lives to building the gigantic Ark. Where did he get the supplies? He either already owned them, or he had to purchase them. Look at Abram:

Genesis 13:1-2 (NLT) "¹ So Abram left Egypt and traveled north into the Negev, along with his wife and Lot and all that they owned. ² (Abram was very rich in livestock, silver, and gold.)"

Let's look at Joseph, Abram's (Abraham) great-grandson:

Genesis 39:2 (KJV) "And the LORD was with Joseph, and he was a prosperous man; and he was in the house of his master the Egyptian."

Proof 3:

When the Lord is with a man, whatever he does prospers. It seems God wants His people to prosper.

Psalms 1:3 (KJV) "And he shall be like a tree planted by the rivers of water, that bringeth forth his fruit in his season;

his leaf also shall not wither; and whatsoever he doeth shall prosper."

Look at this scripture.

Psalms 35:27 (KJV) "Let them shout for joy, and be glad, that favour my righteous cause: yea, let them say continually, Let the LORD be magnified, which hath pleasure in the prosperity of his servant."

Prosperity - h7965. שָׁלוֹם šâlôm; or שָׁלֹם shalom; from 7999; safe, i.e. (figuratively) well, happy, friendly; also (abstractly) welfare, i.e. health, prosperity, peace: — x do, familiar, x fare, favour, + friend, x great, (good) health, (x perfect, such as be at) peace(-able, -ably), prosper(-ity, -ous), rest, safe(-ty), salute, welfare, (x all is, be) well, x wholly.

AV (236) - peace 175, well 14, peaceably 9, welfare 5, salute + h7592 4, prosperity 4, did 3, safe 3, health 2, peaceable 2, misc 15;

3 John 1:2 (KJV) "Beloved, I wish above all things that thou mayest prosper and be in health, even as thy soul prospereth."

g2137. εὐοδόω euodoō; from a compound of 2095 and 3598; to help on the road, i.e. (passively) succeed in reaching; figuratively, to succeed in business affairs: — (have a) prosper(-ous journey).

AV (4) - prosper 3, have a prosperous journey 1; to grant a prosperous and expeditious journey, to lead by a direct and easy wayto grant a successful issue, to cause to prosperto prosper, be successful

Many people—and maybe some reading this little book—still don't believe that God wants us to prosper, even though we have proven this over and over in this chapter. The reason many Christians still believe in the poverty of Christians is because of these three reasons:

1. **They still believe the lie of the enemy: that money and wealth are evil.**

1 Timothy 6:10 (KJV) "For the love of money is the root of all evil: which while some coveted after, they have

erred from the faith and pierced themselves through with many sorrows."

Notice the Bible says the "love of money...", not "money" is the root of all evil.

2. People believe it's wrong for God's people to prosper—and right for evil people to have all the wealth.

Let's look at *Psalms 73:1–12*, where Asaph wrestles with seeing the prosperity of the wicked. He describes how they seem to live in ease, flaunting their riches while mocking God. But later in the chapter, he discovers their end is destruction and that true inheritance is in God's presence. How did the wicked get it? The answer is revealed in:

Luke 4:5–6 when Satan tells Jesus that all the kingdoms and glory of the world were handed over to him, and he can give them to whomever he chooses.

Genesis 1:26 when God originally gave man dominion over the earth.

Genesis 2:8–13 in the Garden, God surrounded Adam with resources like gold and precious stones, showing His intent for mankind to live in abundance.

The wealth transfer happened when Adam forfeited it through sin, giving authority to Satan. But through Christ, the *last Adam*, that dominion and prosperity are being restored to the faithful.

3. Christians believe that if God wants them to have money, God is responsible.

Deuteronomy 8:18; Joshua 1:8; 3 John 1:2; Genesis 12:1-4; Genesis 13:2; Job 36:12; Psalms 1:1-3

I want to prove one more thing. Jesus told the disciples to pray the Lord's prayer which says:

Matthew 6:10 (KJV) "Thy kingdom come. Thy will be done in earth, as it is in heaven."

No one will argue that there is no poverty in Heaven. Even the most staunch anti-prosperity Christians surely believe that God has prosperity in Heaven. Jesus told us to pray that God's will be done on earth as it is in Heaven. So, if there is wealth in Heaven, it must be God's will. And if we are to pray that God's will be done on earth, then we should also pray for wealth on earth.

Proof #4:

God's children should have wealth on earth because their Father has wealth in Heaven. Read how the Apostle John describes Heaven in the Book of Revelation:

Revelation 21:16-20 (NLT) "16 When he measured it, he found it was a square, as wide as it was long. In fact, its length and width and height were each 1,400 miles. 17 Then he measured the walls and found them to be 216 feet thick (according to the human standard used by the angel). 18 The wall was made of jasper, and the city was pure gold, as clear as glass. 19 The wall of the city was built on foundation stones inlaid with twelve precious stones: the first was jasper, the second sapphire, the third agate, the fourth emerald, 20 the fifth onyx, the sixth carnelian, the seventh chrysolite, the eighth beryl, the ninth topaz, the tenth chrysoprase, the eleventh jacinth, the twelfth amethyst."

In today's economy, what would be the approximate value of the streets of gold? If Heaven were 1,500 square miles of solid gold, one foot deep—based on current market prices—it would cost approximately $1.5

quadrillion dollars at an average price of $2,900 per ounce. And just one gate of pearls would be valued at around $6 trillion.

We must conclude that God is not against wealth for His people. He actually promotes it and created all things for us, His children, to enjoy.

1 Timothy 6:17-18 (KJV) "[17] Charge them that are rich in this world, that they be not highminded, nor trust in uncertain riches, but in the living God, who giveth us richly all things to enjoy; [18] That they do good, that they be rich in good works, ready to distribute, willing to communicate;"

WHAT I'M BELIEVING FOR

DATE

S M T W T F S

PEN YOUR FAITH-FILLED EXPECTATIONS AND LET YOUR VISION TAKE SHAPE

WRITE THE VISION AND MAKE IT PLAIN:

_____
_____
_____

WHAT SCRIPTURE ARE YOU STANDING ON FOR WHAT YOU'RE BELIEVING FOR:

_____
_____
_____
_____

HOW AM I DEMONSTRATING THAT I BELIEVE I RECEIVED:

Manifestation Date _____ / _____ / _____

JOURNAL & NOTES

daily notes   date:

WHAT I'M BELIEVING FOR

DATE

S M T W T F S

PEN YOUR FAITH-FILLED EXPECTATIONS AND LET YOUR VISION TAKE SHAPE

WRITE THE VISION AND MAKE IT PLAIN:

WHAT SCRIPTURE ARE YOU STANDING ON FOR WHAT YOU'RE BELIEVING FOR:

HOW AM I DEMONSTRATING THAT I BELIEVE I RECEIVED:

Manifestation Date ___ / ___ / ___

JOURNAL & NOTES

daily notes   *date:*

WHAT I OWE

WHO DO YOU OWE: (PERSON OR COMPANY)

BALANCE:

PAYMENT PLAN: WEEKLY OR MONTHLY

AMOUNT WEEKLY OR MONTHLY:

DATE	PAYMENT	NEW BALANCE

DATE PAID OFF:

daily notes *date:*

WHAT I OWE

WHO DO YOU OWE: (PERSON OR COMPANY)

BALANCE:

PAYMENT PLAN: WEEKLY   OR   MONTHLY

AMOUNT WEEKLY OR MONTHLY:

DATE	PAYMENT	NEW BALANCE

DATE PAID OFF:

daily notes *date:*

WHAT I OWE

WHO DO YOU OWE: (PERSON OR COMPANY)

BALANCE:

PAYMENT PLAN: WEEKLY   OR   MONTHLY

AMOUNT WEEKLY OR MONTHLY:

DATE	PAYMENT	NEW BALANCE

DATE PAID OFF:

daily notes   *date:*

WHAT I OWE

WHO DO YOU OWE: (PERSON OR COMPANY)

BALANCE:

PAYMENT PLAN: WEEKLY   OR   MONTHLY

AMOUNT WEEKLY OR MONTHLY:

DATE	PAYMENT	NEW BALANCE

DATE PAID OFF:

daily notes *date:*

WHAT I OWE

WHO DO YOU OWE: (PERSON OR COMPANY)

BALANCE:

PAYMENT PLAN: WEEKLY OR MONTHLY

AMOUNT WEEKLY OR MONTHLY:

DATE	PAYMENT	NEW BALANCE

DATE PAID OFF:

daily notes   date:

daily notes *date*

NOTES

daily notes — *date:*

daily notes *date:*

daily notes   *date:*

daily notes   date:

daily notes   *date:*

KINGDONOMICS
KINGDOM ECONOMICS

STEP 1 
Born Again
Romans 10:9

STEP 2 
Discipled in Righteousness
What's right? Paying debts, no cutting corners, stop all illegal activity.
Tithing Malachi 3:8 under Discipleship
Matthew 6:33
Proverbs 22:7

STEP 3 
Use Your Faith to Bring in Money OR Items
Significant Seed Sowing
Galatians 6:7
Mark 11:24

STEP 4 
Receive Favor!
Proverbs 22:1

STEP 5 
Experience the Double Portion
Exodus 16:22

STEP 6 
Access Money for the Mission
Matthew 28:19

STEP 7 
Get the overflow and become debt free
John 10:10

STEP 8 
Finance the Kingdom and Generosity to Others
2 Corinthians 9:7-11

© 2025 Pastor Rondy Long Jr. No part of this document may be reproduced or transmitted in any form or by any means, electronic or mechanical, including photocopying, or by any information storage and retrieval system, without written permission of the publisher.

Salvation

Make sure that you are born again! **Pray this Prayer:**

Dear Jesus, I ask You to come into my heart to be my boss and savior. Forgive me for all the mess that I have made. Forgive me for all my sins. I have made so many mistakes, and now, Lord, I am willing to turn from that life and embrace the new life that You have promised to all who turn to You. I believe that You died and rose from the dead for my sins, faults, and mistakes. I confess with my mouth that you are now Lord of my life and I belong to You. Thank you, Lord Jesus, for saving me. Amen.

1. If you are confused about Salvation, purchase our book "The SAT: Salvation Accuracy Test" at www.lastgenerationpublishing.com

2. Get all known sins out of your life, especially anything that causes you to be in a "lifestyle of sin."
3. Find, follow, and fulfill your divine purpose and assignment.
4. Share the Gospel with unbelievers and share the Rapture Revelation book with other Christians.
5. Pray that you are counted worthy to escape the tribulation by being ready to go in the Rapture.

Luke 21:36 (KJV) "Watch ye therefore, and pray always, that ye may be accounted worthy to escape all these things that shall come to pass, and to stand before the Son of man."

Pray this Prayer

Dear Heavenly Father, I know you know when Jesus will rapture the Church. Lord, help me to be ready when He returns. Remove any person, object, idol, philosophy, behavior, or anything that will hinder me from being ready when the Rapture occurs. I know I will never actually deserve anything that You do for me because you saved me from my sins when I didn't deserve them. But I pray as Jesus instructed us; I pray that I am "accounted worthy" to escape. Lord, I want to be ready. I don't want to be left behind. In Jesus' name, we pray, Amen!

Get Your Kingdom Products
www.LastGenerationPublishing.com

LISTEN TO THE ENTIRE SERIES ON MP3

KINGDONOMICS

KINDONOMICS CENTERS AROUND THE CONCEPT OF REBRANDING YOUR MONEY IMAGE. WHAT IS YOUR CURRENT MONEY IMAGE? WHAT IS YOUR INNER DIALOGUE ABOUT MONEY AND WEALTH? THIS 8-PART SEGMENT, OF THE LARGER SERIES, WILL HELP DISCOVER HOW GOD PURPOSES US TO REBRAND OUR IDENTITY WITH MONEY.

LastGenerationPublishing.com

About the Author

Rondy Long was born in Charlotte, NC where he miraculously accepted Christ at the age of six years old. He read through most of the New Testament by the age of 7 and began evangelizing his neighborhood. His family then moved to Houston, TX at age eight and he answered the call to preach at age thirteen. He and Regina met two years later in the tenth grade. They dated five years before marrying.

Rondy attended the University of North Texas in Denton, Texas and graduated with Bachelors in Communications. He is the founder of Last Generation Ministries and Kingdom Church of Houston. With over 39 years of experience in the ministry, he has helped many come to know Jesus, and has trained many to work in ministry.

Waiting, Dating, & Mating was his first book. The SAT: Are You Really Saved? Is his second book of several books.

To contact: Email kingdomchurchofhouston@gmail.com
or call at 1-888-879-8189.
Last Generation Ministries Website
www.lastgenerationpublishing.com

www.ingramcontent.com/pod-product-compliance
Lightning Source LLC
Chambersburg PA
CBHW070847160426
43192CB00012B/2342